CHULA

BY
AMANDA
ALCÁNTARA

Chula Copyright © 2019 Amanda Alcantara

www.amandaalcantara.com
Email: contact@amandaalcantara.com

Cover art and design:
Tania Guerra (www.taniaque.com)

Editorial team:
Isabelia Herrera and Jacqueline Jiménez Polanco

Author headshot (page 107):
Emmanuel Abreu

ISBN-13: 978-0-578-46043-7

A mi buelita Álida, te extraño.

Table of Contents

Intro

Recently, I mentioned to someone that though I was born in the
United States, I was raised in the Dominican Republic. My first
language was Spanish. And I came here a los 15, casi 16 años.
They looked at me surprised, telling me I give the impression of
someone who was born and raised here.

It's not the first time I've heard that. When I moved here, I
coped by forgetting – by attempting to let go. I just wanted to fit
in at my new high school, aterrizar bien.

I had to survive. Assimilate.

I slowly stopped talking to my friends in the D.R., stopped
following their lives as they approached graduation, and stopped
paying attention to the chismes del colegio. The entire thing was
too painful. So, rather than continue missing home – missing my
friends – I suppressed all those feelings and resolved to build a
new life here. I got myself a high school sweetheart —un
colombiano de Medellín who was also a recent immigrant — and
went off to chase un sueño.

And I did all of this without self-awareness. Without knowing I
was actively letting go. It sort of just happened. At that time in
my life, I even stopped writing for a few months, which was the
very thing that had helped me survive.

This book is an attempt to rescue my own history, that history,
and other histories. It's an attempt to rescue the parts of myself
that I've hidden, stored away in boxes under my bed, and an
attempt to revisit the life I had left behind in the privacy of my
journal pages. It's an attempt to share and make sense of the

parts of me that aren't hidden, that are inevitably obvious in my face, in my voice, and in my skin. And above all, it's a reivindicación de quien soy y la niña y adolescente que una vez fui.

While this work is autobiographical, it does include some imaginative elements. But it is all inspired by a true story – my true story.

In a way, I've been writing this book my whole life – since I was eight years old, when I first wrote to my "diary" on a journal page and began documenting myself.

Through it all though – through what happened to me in high school while I tried letting go – I never actually changed. Even as I struggled to make friends, con de todo, I never stopped being this big-mouthed, joyous, Spanglish-speaking, reguetón-dancing caribeña that the world didn't seem to have space for.

Today, things are very different for me in terms of the relationship I have con el país que me vió crecer y que fue mi hogar. I go back to the Dominican Republic often. I rekindled my friendships with people there, developing a closeness that miles cannot sever. I've embraced being ni de aquí ni de allá, living on a border and embodying una frontera, like so many of us do.

At 28, yo he sufrido pero también he disfrutado. It's been an interesting life, a grand one, parts of which I'm excited and humbled to share with you all.

En un mundo donde me dicen que soy marginal, aquí recuerdo que mi centro soy yo.

Gracias to my mom, Carmen, for buying me all those books and encouraging me to read. Also, to my madrina Dionis for getting me my first journal when I was seven years old. And to my sister Yesenia, for taking care of me, even when she didn't have to.

A special thanks to Josefina Báez por las tizanas, las enseñanzas de Ay Ombe Theatre, y por *Dominicanish*. To Alicia Anabel Santos for motivating so many women to write, reminding us that our stories matter. And to Sandra Guzmán, for opening her beautiful home to me in Luquillo, Puerto Rico, where I began completing this project.

And last but not least, thanks to my inner child for sticking around even when I forgot she was there.

"This is for colored girls who have considered suicide, but are moving to the ends of their own rainbows." - Ntozake Shange

Bom bom baby
Bom bom
Rollercoaster
Swing swing baby
I'll never let you go

When I came to the U.S., I tried to learn games other kids played here. This is a song I tried to learn...today, I still can't remember the whole thing.

When I was growing up, in the summertime, Mami would always send me and my sister over to our grandparents' house in West New York, NJ from Santiago. They've been there since the 70's.

I remember finding my very first passport and it had three stamps on it, from before I could even walk – before we moved permanently (dique permanently) to the D.R. when I was three years old.

Chimi chimi
Coco pow
Chimi chimi pow

Dice la canción.

In the end, it didn't matter if I learned the whole thing; I always returned to the D.R. before the end of the summer. And I preferred the Dominican songs anyway, like "pollito pleibi," "yo tengo un novio," y así sucesivamente. (I never liked la que dice "arroz con leche" though.)

My grandparents were probably one of the first Dominican families to move to West New York. Primero fue mi abuelo quien comenzó su viaje por Puerto Rico, then my grandmother and her four kids followed. And little by little, extended family started showing up.

In the U.S., everyone had to work. At the time, it was a mostly Cuban town where people worked in the garment industry. My grandparents rented a tiny two-bedroom apartment where my cousin still lives to this day, though both of my grandparents already passed away. They just sold the building, but my cousin is holding onto it since it's rent-controlled, and the town se está llenando de gringos. So ya tú sabes que it's becoming a coveted place to live.

In school, I always used to brag about the summer I spent in the United States. I showed off my language skills during English lessons and would always compare the two countries. "The U.S. has clean bathrooms, no como aquí."

I was kind of obnoxious. Yo no me hubiera aguantado a mí misma en el colegio.

Pero cuando me preguntaban cuál país me gustaba más, siempre decía la República Dominicana. Específicamente Santiago.

Aprendí de los adultos que el tráfico de la capital es insoportable and even though I had never been, I used to mimic everything my mom did. "A mí no me gusta la capital. Demasiada gente."

Mami didn't like the U.S. either; that's why she left when she divorced my dad. We ended up in the D.R. by the time I was 3, so my first language was Spanish. Still, being "American," with access to U.S. dollars and fluency in English, gave Mami an entry point into things in the D.R. she didn't have growing up. She no longer had to live en Nibaje or Laguna Prieta where my buelita Álida was from, and she could afford to move up and give me and my sister a better life.

Y ella se fajó trabajando to put me and my sister through private school, with child support from just one of our two fathers. Whenever we visited other, better-off cousins, I remembered how much we lacked. And Mami complained about not having money all the time.

Still, she managed to send us to private school in the D.R. and to make sure we had everything she didn't.

We tried about five different schools (a different one every year) before finding the right fit. We changed schools either because they were too expensive, or because one time, one of the teachers became infatuated with my older sister. She has light eyes, light skin, and light-colored hair like her dad. They called her "una niña bella," and it was both a blessing and a curse.

Eventually, Mami found the perfect school when I was in 7th grade. It was a new school with the promise of affordability and a good education. Looking back, I suppose the owner and principal didn't lie. There were about 40 students in each classroom and the school taught all types of subjects, from French to art. They also had a writing competition that I won. I still remember how shocked and excited I was when they called my name.

I loved it. I had amiguitas who changed to this school from other schools, who I had met after I turned nine. I barely spent summers en el país though. It was like some reverse shit where we actually went to the U.S. to visit Buelita and not the other way around.

During our summers in the U.S., my tía would get us our school uniforms to take back to the D.R. We wore used clothes the entire time and saved all the new outfits to them show off back home. In the D.R., we couldn't afford the clothes from La Plaza Zona Rosa or the fancy stores. It was cheaper to buy them on

13

Bergenline Ave. at Señor Barato or E.J. Roberts, then look all fresh in the D.R.

I'd love the plane ride back home with las azafatas. They always looked like these magical women with high heels who put video games on for you, gave you a ton of sweet snacks, and tended to all your needs.

And in the D.R., I had todas mis amiguitas, Mami had a car which we didn't have in the U.S. and I could play outside en el medio de la calle en la Fernando Valerio o el Ensueño o en los lugares donde mis amiguitas vivían, and just run out of the way when cars came. One time, I almost got hit by a car, which stopped right as its front hood was by my tiny stomach. Another time, I did actually get hit montando motocicleta.

We were visiting una tía mía que tenía una casa y un patio grandísimo. I always liked visiting her house, but only for the backyard. Inside, everything was so clean, it didn't feel like a space for me.

The older kids who usually played with my sister were teaching me how to ride the motocicleta. I was six, and I already knew how to ride a bike, but this one had plastic decorations all over it to make it look like a pasola, even though you still had to pedal.

It all happened so fast. When I was finally riding it, I reached an intersection, and una jeepeta was coming towards me. All I had to do was stop, but the frenos were too far for my little fingers to reach. I heard my sister scream, "¡Dale pa'tra'! ¡Dale pa'tra'!"

Apparently, you could also pedal backwards to brake, but I didn't react fast enough, and as the car hit me from the left side, someone yelled, "¡Ay la mató!"

I don't remember much from there, except waking up in my tía's pristine kitchen, with everyone around me, my mom pressing something wet on my head. My sister was crying. Later, Mami would tell me the driver was there too, having a panic attack.

"Ella 'ta bien," I heard someone say, as I woke up. The bike was so big, la jeepeta barely touched me.

Now we just laugh at the whole thing. Good times.

Nunca seré fina pero tampoco soy sencilla
bailando reguetón desde niña
liberación en las marquesinas

I'm a Libra
catch me en la esquina
spreading fliers, handing out ideas
Dudes tryna look back at it like I'm Trina
Lip gloss popping, call me Lil Dita
La revolución va tai encendía
Fuego en la cintura y Fuego a la oligarquía
Soy puta pero picky, call me fresita
Sepo más rico que el postre de su marida
Los pongo en cuclilla a comer gratis, así le llenó la barriga
Now you can call me Mother Teresa

But for real tho, let me reintroduce myself
Soy Amanda Alcántara con acento en la A
La palabrista
La que se hacía llamar Radical Latina
La que confunden de niña teniendo de reina la pinta
La que se inventa frases porque vive entre 2 lenguas y 5 vidas
Hija hermana puta santa y amiga
Y bésame la mano
Que también soy tu madrina
La que se ve buena aunque no corre ni una milla
That bitch u hate cuz u assumed she problematic but she still
about freedom
Más que Frida, yo soy la de artes de autocrítica
Tú te crees woke pero sigues a las mases. Yo sigo a la vida
I'm the spirit to ur Sprite
The electricity pa tus pilas
The one that hits u a escondidas
Y cuando se va, se siente
Emotional diva
Unconventional liricista
Underestimated leader
Watching me walk away es un privilegio para tus ojos

16

Y un deseo pa tu boquita
Me prefieren muerta porque mi boca es muy grande pa sus ideas
vendidas
pero esta rosa no se marchita
Call me Margarita
Y te lo repito por si se te olvida
Nunca seré fina pero tampoco soy sencilla.

This is where I tell you where my parents met.

Their story no es una cosa del otro mundo. It wasn't some super romantic story. There wasn't a big gesture. Mami already had a kid. And Papi tambien tenía una mujer y dos hijos de dos mujeres distintas.

And that complicated shit makes it more relatable than those big stories of how people meet ¡Dime que no! The ones where they were in love for years and ended up together finally because one person never gave up. The ones where it was love at first sight. The ones where they ran away from home.

Nah. My parents met through mutuals and sealed it on the dance floor. Two messy people aficiándose uno del otro in their mid-20's and bringing all their baggage with them.

By that time, my mom had already left her first husband and become a single mom. My sister's dad is un dominicano with light eyes and light skin. "Un tipo buenmozo," people would tell her when they met him. She met him and left my grandparents' house when she had barely turned 18. Today, I'm told my grandparents were very strict, and even though they were en el país del libertinaje, marrying was still the easiest way for a young girl to escape an abusive home. Turns out where she ended up wasn't very different than her parents' place.

My dad still had hair when he met her after she had gone through all that. He had one of those 80's fros. I haven't seen many pictures of him from his past, except some where he's carrying me. He's the life of the party, always has been. And when he starts drinking, he can't stop until the sun comes out and people start leaving. One time, he wanted to drop me off in the old

18

building where him and Mami lived and where my cousin stayed, but he stopped a block away instead. "Si me ven por allá, después todo el mundo me quiere saludar y no dejan que me vaya."

His face is printed on mine, to the point where Facebook face recognition tags us in each other's photos. Sometimes older people in the family see me and I figure they must see him, since they almost immediately ask, "¿Y tu papá cómo está?"

"Bien, tú sabes, con su mujer y sus hijos en Pensilvania."

He's popular af. Siempre haciendo un can. That entire side of the family is like that, and whenever I visit, I can expect to have a Presidente in my hand as soon as I walk in. I also look like my cousins on that side too – light brown skin con pelo largo. I always have a fun time when I'm with them.

Mami had those big pollinas back when they met. The poufy ones that Mami's favorite artists had – Whitney Houston and Gloria Estefan. She played them all the time en la casa. And Mami always gets confused for cubana in the U.S., especially in Hudson County.

When she's in the D.R., la gente le dice que tiene aire de que viaja, "por tu piel."

Mami has also always been llenita and is on a perpetual diet since forever.

But her thickness is what draws people, what makes her cheeks lift up and stand out when she smiles. It makes her beauty de película, like Marilyn Monroe. That smile of hers has always been so charming. One time, she won a Goya beauty pageant and she got to travel to Puerto Rico.

She's the only one in the family who returned to live in Santiago and always tells the story of how a famous merenguero was in love with her, so he'd invite her to his parties. This was all while she had us and was single for a while, living in the D.R. and finally free.

I've seen her in action. Incluso now, she gets guys trying to hook up with her and men hitting on her when we go out. Recently, she ended a relationship and she has that new recently broken-up glow. "Los hombres no sirven, uno tiene que hacer las cosas sola," she says.

They're both light-skinned, my parents. My sister Liz has thin straight hair with green eyes and also light skin. En el colegio le decían la gringa. Y cuando llegué yo, yo era la morenita de la casa. I was blessed by the ancestors. They were like, "¡Tituá! Esta va a ser de piel india, pa' recordarle a ustedes de donde son, coño."

Y nací yo. I came out crying. My mom says the doctors were shocked by how loud I was. Since I was a baby, I've had a big-ass mouth.

When I was born, my tía was with my mami. I was premature; I was supposed to be a Halloween baby, but was born at the end of September. Mi tía helped pick all of our names and she chose mine (Thank God; me querían poner Leslie). Apparently, everyone thought Amanda Alcántara sounded poetic, important, and it rhymed. I love that shit. Later on, Mami would regret not naming me Amanda Miguel como la cantante because I happened to be born el día de San Miguel. I love that shit too.

My parents were living in the U.S. when I was born. Mami had returned so Papi could get his visa and she could have his kid.

When I was three, Mami decided she wanted to leave the U.S.

"Estos hombres no sirven," I can picture her thinking, again. So agarró a sus dos muchachas y se fue.

Mami tells me my dad wasn't in the hospital with her when I was born. He was en el patio del edificio, celebrando on that September evening, with his friends and some bottles of beer.

As I've gotten older, I've started to look more and more like my mom. Her big smile, lifted cheeks.

I guess I see myself in both of them.

I'm the treasure born entre la samba y el vodou
Entre el moro y el mangú
Soy la huella de mis ancestros
Que cura al mundo del fukú
Las caricias de mi abuela llegan más lejos que tu I love u
Soy más fuerte que Gokú
Más valiente que el imperio de Estados U
Más fluyente que un haiku
We rely on resilience and we still better than u boo
Soy Amaru y tú no eres más que un frontú

Soy de la isla
Quisqueya la bella
Brown y Negra
I am the truth.

Todos los domingos cocino yó
Plátano Maduro con salchichón
Viene un policía y me pide un chin
Saca la pistola y me dice así
Uno
Ahí y ahí
Dos
Ahí y ahí
Tres
Ahí y ahí
Cuatro
Ahí y ahí
Cinco
Ahí y ahí

Y así susesivamente iba otra canción, de las dominicanas, that
I'd sing de chiquitita.

I used to hate this one, pero por lo menos me la sabía. I just
didn't understand cuál era el show con el salchichón, y por qué
uno bailaba así.

I remember I learned this song when I lived en la Fernando
Valerio. There I met el primer noviecito mío. Or enamorado. Or
this kid I liked. Daniel.

I was 8 or 9.

We used to go to the same school too. But in school I couldn't
call him Daniel. Había que decirle otro nombre. I think it was
something to do with his papers. Or maybe Daniel was a
nickname.

He never did want to be my official "noviecito." One time, I had a dream that I was in this giant white space, and that I knew I was dreaming. In the dream, I thought, "OMG, I can have sex without consequences and finally figure out what the heck it's all about." So I tried to, I summoned him, but I had no idea what I was doing or what was what; we kind of just stood there, then I summoned him away and woke up.

I guess I had to know what sex actually was before doing it in a dream.

La Fernando Valerio was a neighborhood a bit further away than usual from the center of Santiago, but we had a house to ourselves and a ton of pets. We owned a dog, chickens, and little birds. My sister really loved pets and my mom indulged her until we got bored.

There, I used to play with this girl who was a year younger than me and lived across the street. We also played with him and some other boys.

In my first-ever diary entry, that I ever actually wrote, ever in my whole life, I had written, "Dear Diore, y love and like Daniel" (lovely typos and all). He had lived in the United States too. He also had this "pelo bueno" that was so coveted in our culture. It was shiny, light brown, and reached his ears. He had this mancha on his face too: a brown spot right on his cheek. His skin was about the same color as mine.

One time, he grabbed me and took me to a side street. I remember fighting him off. I mean, I was scared and knew that I didn't want this, but I was supposed to want it, right? The entire thing was so confusing.

24

I tried to run, but he was faster. As he held me, he gave another boy who passed by el signo de singar, which I had just learned too. Basically, you put your index finger into a circle formed by the index and thumb of the opposite hand. He then started humping me —with my clothes on— and trying to kiss me. I fought him off, feeling so ashamed. Eventually he let me go. I can't remember much, except his blob on my face, his saliva everywhere, and his stinky breath.

I went home, angry.

My first love. He didn't like me, but he liked me like that, so maybe he did like me.

When that happened, I guess he tried to have sex with me too. But cuz he's a boy, he didn't need a dream. He had permission to do it in real life. And he didn't even need consent.

I guess he too had to know what sex actually was before doing it to someone, forcefully.

Stgo, 9 de Septiembre, 1999

Dear Diore,

y want you to ceap this secret y ♥ love ♥ and like ♥ Daniel ♥
and y think he likes me to but isn't he ♥
cute ♥. The cutest one is ♥ Daniel ♥

My Spanish is an Afroindigenous creolized Cibao song which
my buelita sang as if it was her favorite bolero.

She danced to the beat of her own drums with her words
Palabreando
Kelokeando
Ando buscando
El jengibre pai mai de amore
Saboreando
Buscando el canto
Que lo boté sin querer
Celia Cruzeando
Con estos pesitos
Rimando throughout the day

When my buelita uttered English words it sounded like un
merengue ripiao
Turning Shop Rite into chorai
Pathmark into pajmai
Taiget fanfea vivaporú
When I lived with her
I didn't go to P.S. number 1
I went to la nombel guan

Slicing through centuries of English and Spanish colonialism
Her tongue was a machete
Su lengua era un colín afilao
(Resistance is in her tongue)
Resistance was spelled in every vowel emanating from her
mouth
What's more beautiful than that?

Let me tell you,
With all the work I put in,
if I was whiter, I'd be famous
If I was taller, I'd be popular
If I was male, I'd be rich
But I'm a petite and brown bitch
Tall in flyness, I go high, intergalactic bliss
So much u try to ignore that I exist
Tryna wear my skin
But I am not trying to Get Out
The whole Earth is my crib
Her gravity is her way of loving me
And she loved me so much that I barely made it past 5 feet
U may be taller but I'm closer to divinity
My mama is the OG your white Mami is the original thief
And yet I gotchu wanting to suck on my clit
But u can't colonize the lands of my body
I come with fury like a tsunami
U can't handle my waters bout to have you drowning
Lips so fresh u think u breathing
Tryna force me to call u papi

Hm

New York

This city weighs heavy on my chest, an unwanted burden and yet the place I've turned into my home. Sometimes Santiago weighed heavy on me, too. I remember afternoons in the back of Mami's Honda driving by the Estrella Sadhalá, trees mixed in with two-story buildings, the entire weight of life on my shoulders and my tween soul. When the sun sets, I feel nostalgic, death looming and coming closer as every day falls. And I think of those moments. Of my face against the glass window, savoring that feeling. When I remember that, every day, and with every passing year, I think maybe I'm getting closer to uncovering what that feeling is. That nagging. That longing. Miradas perdidas and sore hearts from swelling too much. Sore cheeks from smiling too hard, now awaiting salty tears. Maybe I'll become wiser and understand it and the pain en mi pecho will dissipate with life.

Today I sit on this subway train, breathing through it. Having just said goodbye to my friends. Another night out that comes to an end. And I think that the opposite is true. The wiser I become, the heavier the feeling weighs.

I remember one time when I was like 6, I pretended to fall asleep on a rocking chair outside la casa de mi tía. Like I said, I wasn't asleep, I was pretending. But the day had already ended and I think I longed for something. They tried tickling me so I could stop pretending, and I held my laughter in, trying to keep my lips pursed and my eyes shut. Finally, one of my tíos picked me up and carried me upstairs. I can't remember being placed on the bed, or anything more after he picked me up. I'm sure I fell asleep in his arms, feeling loved.

"Just a girl"

A regular girl living in this world, that's all she is. A girl with long dark hair. A girl with brown eyes under a pair of glasses that make her feel weak. A girl with about 6 extra pounds that anorexic models make her feel like those 6 pounds were 12. A girl seeking for a place where her perfect curves and her unique mind are fully accepted. That's all she is. A girl with many secrets. A girl who has broken many hearts but whose heart has never been broken. A girl whose heart has never been broken by someone else because she would rather do it herself than have someone else break it. A girl with a mom, a sister, and a dad that she wishes she could hate. All she is is a simple pretty girl living in the world. A girl with only one best friend and about 76 friends on her "MySpace." A girl who thinks has great self-esteem but sometimes, just sometimes, she wishes to be someone else. Sometimes she even wishes to be more beautiful, she wishes to stop keeping her legs closed and disrespect herself so that guys stop wanting her and just take her. Sometimes, she goes up to the rooftop, and looks down while thinking about jumping, to see if maybe, just maybe, she can find a place just for her.

---

*16 years old, 5 months after arriving to the U.S.

An ode to my stretch marks

You broke into my skin
As if ripping open a gift box
Delivering me into womanhood
At the age of 12

A gift I didn't want
A warning of the scars this body would endure
Before I was too skinny
And then you came
And so came
tíos and cousins who would look with eyes I didn't understand
Notes passed to me in the bus by older men
This niña is a mujerón now
I blamed u
I was ashamed of you
They made me hate you

So today I reclaim u

You are more than war scars of my womanhood
You are a painting in my flesh as I became abundant and
eventually you'd engulf my hips
show up in my stomach and arms and calves too
Stretching to infinity
Reminding me that a body cannot comprehend a soul
But its walls will expand beyond their limit to be the home to so
much life.
Drawing maps in my brown skin
As if ocean waves were breaking through
Roots reminding me of my home when the winter turns me pale
My grandma could stretch a meal to feed everyone with so little
And you, you stretch
you stretch to hold such greatness.

Buelita's Hands

I remember how her hand felt on my cheek.

Her soft, wrinkly, dark caramel hand. She smelled like agua florida y polvo maja. It wasn't until later in life when I went to buy agua florida and recognized the light, familiar scent that I learned what the heck she was even wearing. Y el bendito polvo maja; it was common for abuelas to use that thing.

Why did I never take the time to ask her about her life? Visiting her always felt like a burden, and now I have an altar with her picture.

Que hipocresía.

Kids need to fucking respect their elders, man. I used to hate visiting her at el home. It smelled like poop, processed food, and old people. "¿Dónde tan mi cuaito?" she would ask. With it, she could pay a lady to dye her hair, another one to do her nails, all while playing bingo in the 5th floor of el home.

I was perreando solita one time at home, just for fun, in the casa in Santiago, and got taken aback when she told me que parecía un cuero. I was so ashamed, I didn't understand half the lyrics at the time, so I didn't fully know what she even meant.

I did eventually become a cuero later on, though. Pero I know it's okay. A su manera, ella tampoco era fácil.

Stgo, 17 de junio, 2006*

Dear Diary,

I've decided to lose my virginity with Henry. I mean life doesn't make any sense anyways, I mean since about 3 months I've noticed that, and if love makes me happy, why wait? Besides, I'm going to use protection.

And I feel like being free, so I don't care about morals. What morals? I mean, I'm going to suffer anyways 'cause that is what life is about and I might as well suffer for something good.

I feel like escaping just like in the song "quiero escapar" or something de Kudai.

And I was crying like hell yesterday afternoon, so I let it all out and now I know what I want and not what other people want.

Oh! And I'm going to Amaprosan today, mom thinks I'm going with Patricia, but it's not true, I'm going with Henry.

---

*15 years old, 3 months before leaving to the U.S.

Before moving to the United States, there is one thing I knew I had to do: lose my virginity.

I was 15 and had held on to mi virginidad like a good, Bible-reading, churchgoing Catholic girl. But something in me knew survival where I was going was different than survival in the Dominican Republic. I was going to el país del libertinaje, y en "Nueva York," las muchachas no eran fáciles. So, como dicen los gringos, it was time to pop the cherry.

At that point, I had known for months that I was coming to the U.S. and my explorations had reached a peak. Fue como si to'a la porquería que había aprendido sobre womanhood y respect didn't matter anymore.

"Amanda, agárrate con to el mundo," was the advice one of my friends gave me. Both her and I knew que ya yo me iba y mi reputación no importaba. So agarrarme con to los jovenes lindos that I wanted to I did. Me volví una puta by my own standards. Hasta tuve un día en que me chulié a tres muchachos del colegio back to back (not at the same time por si acaso). No sex though, not even close. Just besitos and grinding with clothes on, perreo full, while constantly moving their sweaty hands away from my breasts.

Still, it's like my sexual liberation had arrived by way of a one-way ticket to the Yunited States, starting otra vez with nothing but a dark-inked T-shirt with "no cambies" messages that came two years before my actual graduation. I figured I could try to keep thriving as a student, because hopefully at least that I could do, even if I feared going to a place where I had no friends.

So yeah, the first person to find out was my noviecito at the time: Henry.

I say noviecito because it lasted like 2 months, but that shit was intense. I mean, nada más a dos muchachos clueless se les ocurriría dique comenzar un enamoramiento right when one of them was about to leave. But the impossibility of love is what made it fire. And he had a visa and visited the U.S. de vez en cuando too, so maybe it'd work out.

Henry was un muchacho lindo: relatively tall, con hazel eyes, a big smile, tan olive skin, y el pelo thick pero lacio y light brown that you could comb your fingers through. Él se lo peinaba with a little curve at the tip, como Clark Kent or los tipos de las telenovelas. Henry was also from a family kind of like mine: well-off por los dólares que venían de Nueva York, pero todavía pasaban trabajo for some things. He also wasn't del colegio, which made him even more interesting; we met cuz his cousin was in my grade. And cuz I had an even shorter "noviazgo" with his other cousin, though that barely counts cuz we only saw each other twice and never even kissed. I think that situation somehow added to the impossibility of our love too. Él le robó la novia al primo y yo entonces era una novia digna de ser robada.

He was excited when I told him and soooo ready. He had had sex with one other girl before me, so that reassured me that at least one of us would know how this worked. I mean, yo no era bruta. I knew that 1. we needed condoms for some reason 2. que tenía que entrar enterito for it to count and 3. the whole thing supposedly felt good, though according to the porn I had watched, mostly for the guy…she just feels good pleasuring him.

By the time Mami told me we were going to move, I knew it was coming. But it still hurt. I ran into my room and started crying, then told my best friend Ana the next day in school. She didn't act hurt or anything, she just said "I'm not surprised," which made me hurt even more.

The thing is, I had already left one time before in 8th grade. I remember it was during a time when all these terremotos were happening in the D.R. and people suspected we were leaving out of fear, but really, it was something more like my Mami wanting something new, and the possibility of a better education for us.

I was 13. Mami, Liz, and I came to West New York, NJ. We came in January, mid-way through the school year. I remember making friends was the hardest. It was during this time when I also started to believe the whole thing about girls in the U.S. being "faster," or at least some of them. One time, we were in sex ed class and a group of girls sitting in the back was giggling the whole time, then one of them asked if you could get pregnant through anal sex. The teacher said yes.

One time, I was standing in line before going into class and two of the girls from that same group came up to where I was, as one asked the other, "Do you wanna see the new girl?" They looked at me up and down, laughed, and walked away.

I did make friends eventually – another smart dominicana who was one of the best students in class, and a Colombian girl who was mean to both of us but for some reason we let her be. One time, the popular girls invited me to a house party, and I went. The entire time I didn't fit in, and when I did dance, I got made fun of. Then I hung out with them during lunchtime the next day and they asked, pointing to my other friends' table, "Amanda,

36

who do you hang out with – them or us?" I was so confused. You mean to tell me I actually had to choose? So yeah, I never sat with them again.

Everyone was so mean.

In Santiago, I had my best friend who I had known since I was nine, and my other best friend Nilsia. And a ton of other close friends. Though it was mostly the three of us, and we were tight. Las loquitas pero inteligentes del curso. We were loud, dique excéntricas, but fun, and we also got good grades and were part of a lot of the after-school stuff, like me and Nilsia were Girl Scouts. She was also a lead in the marching band when all of us marched in uniforms like proud, young, patriotic yet unofficial soldiers down Las Carreras every 30 de marzo. Ana was an artist, and together we'd decorate the classroom whenever a new month and new theme came up.

Damn, I guess we were low-key nerdy too.

But that's the thing: in the All-American High School Musical I was preparing myself for (again), there wasn't space for teens like us – you were either cool or you weren't. The bully or the bullied.

***

En mi casa, we weren't even the strict kind of Catholics. I remember Mami couldn't have la hostia — the body of Christ — because she had been married by the church then divorced. But we were in a Catholic country. And in a machista world. Body count mattered no matter what. I had been convinced that if I had anything more than one man in my life, I'd be a sullied, unwanted cuero.

Fuck the Catholic church for making me believe that.

So, I invited Henry to my house one afternoon when Mami wasn't there. When I knew she wouldn't be there until later in the evening.

We used the bed in the room my sister had left behind, de tamaño full. And she was living in the U.S. already. There was a lot of natural light in that room, and a mirror facing the bed. In the window by the bed, there was a mango tree that had to get its leaves cut so it wouldn't bust through las persianas. It gave us some privacy. Also, it was the third floor, the last one, so no one could see us.

We started just making out, chuleando.

Eventually, clothes started coming off. When we were completely naked is when things got complicated.

We were both so nervous, I kept waiting for him to be ready and he never was. When I tried helping, he said I was doing it wrong. I asked if this had happened before; he said no.

I tried and tried and tried to fix it, but it didn't work. He was never ready.

I thought he had done this before and I felt embarrassed and angry. And cheated.

In the end, we put on our clothes and said we'd try again.

Days passed and we didn't talk about it. Was I broken? Had it been my fault? He had already done it with someone else; maybe I wasn't performing well.

I finally told one person, someone older. She was a friend's older sister and we became close after I had gone to a Pavel Núñez concert with her. We met at a bar close to my house by la PUCAMAIMA. I wasn't drinking, but we were still there, and it felt super cool.

I knew she already had experience, so I asked.

She told me that that's normal, "¿Cuántos años tiene él? Él estaba nervioso." Then she gave me a condom, and a discount card for una cabaña, and encouraged me to try again somewhere different and nicer.

I never used what she gave me. Henry and I broke up shortly after he had come over. I was almost leaving the country and we couldn't pretend anymore. I was sad, but I knew I wouldn't try doing it with someone else again.

I'd just have to face Memorial High School as I was… an inexperienced, uncool gatica in a world I swore was filled with wolves.

***

I think wanting to lose my virginity became about rejecting what I had been told and taking ownership over an intrinsic part of me. Quise controlar la única cosa que me pertenecía: mi cuerpo y mis decisiones sobre mi cuerpo. Everything else, like where my body would live, was out of my hands.

***

When I did get to the U.S., I wasn't a cool teen; I wasn't nerdy either. My Dominican friend from 8th grade had moved to

39

Pennsylvania, and la colombiana was part of the cool group now, so she never even said hi to me.

I hung out with other recent immigrant kids, got myself a Colombian boyfriend who became my high school sweetheart (and whose parents eventually accepted me but without forgetting to remind me first que su ex era paisa como ellos, y rubia), got good grades but had to fight to be considered a good student, and dabbled in emo style with some cheap black lace gloves and dark eyeliner that I'd somehow match with Easy Pickins clothes from Mami's job. My favorite songs went from the "Locura Automática" reguetón remix to anything by Sin Banderas to The All-American Rejects' "Move Along" to Linkin Park's "Somewhere I Belong" to house music courtesy of el novio. And I prayed to God to make this girl in my English class my new best friend, and God seemed to listen.

Also, I did end up having sex at one point soon after getting to the U.S., right around prom and graduation season. I was seventeen, à la 80's nostalgia. I guess in the end I did do it in a very stereotypical American way.

Alex

Even our bodies travel after we're gone
En la muerte seguimos como el lema, ni de aquí ni de allá
Self-deportation or
Repatriation
only happens after we die, because only in death do we believe
our home is safe.

Amor dominguero

es como cuando el sol sale y uno lo ignora
y pretende levantarse cuando quiera
hasta que te tocan la puerta y te recuerdan que hoy hay misa
como tostones con chuleta frita
porque el arroz es para la semana y hoy no se cocina
como las horas lentas y aburridas que luego hacen falta ya que
pronto se terminan
como la música de la vecina que retumba las paredes
hace temblar el suelo
y sin embargo nos masajea las mejillas
mientras mamá le echa agua a la marquesina

ese sentimiento
esa fuerza del mundo detenido
de un momento sin prisa
tan pasajero pero largo como esta tardecita
de besos
gemidos
y palabras inéditas

Mami told me rooms are sacred and to not let anybody in
So I stay out of cemeteries cuz that's where the dead sleep
I'm tryna live

I don't mess with dark energies
my life is lit
My skin is golden
My land is rich
Se hacen ricos vendiendo el país
Y a nosotros no nos dejan ni un chin
But our spirit still persists

We got joy in our hips
Smile on our lips
Vestío de verde we resist
We keep our pride
Hold on tight
Abundant never dry
In the desert we survive
With the water that's inside
Gushing, I can make u feel
Alive
Let me show what it's like
Got loyalty got royalty inside my DNA
I don't lie
Our people never die
We were the first to inhabit the Earth
U wish u were this fine
Roses in the concrete, we deserve better so we fight
Make us think we're poor Mother Nature knows the truth
DIABLO MAMI TO ESO E TUYO
Sí, the whole world is mine.

Excerpts from "Daydreaming about men." December 2015.

As she got older, the catcalling started.

She remembers first experiencing it when she began taking French classes after school. To get there, she'd have to walk in front of these groups of kids that always hung out by the sidewalk. They were always in the same spot. Whenever she walked by, they would catcall her – a lot. It got worst over time; it almost started to feel like they were waiting for her. They would get in front of her and try to grab her. She eventually started taking el camino largo.

It was confusing, because wasn't she supposed to like this kind of attention?

She was rarely told that she was beautiful by the outside world and was often compared to her rubia older sister Liz. In the D.R., so many people were actually closer to her own complexion. But the lack of whiteness in a predominant sense, made those with proximity to whiteness even more celebrated, adding to her invisibility and to the disturbing fetishizing of her sister. Mami always told her about how she had to tell people from the moment that she was born that if they wanted to play with Liz, they had to play with her too.

She lived in a society where any sign of melanin that her skin showed wasn't celebrated. Instead, people complimented whatever lack of color she had, whether that was her so-called "pelo bueno" (meaning hair that is not considered of African descent) or the fact that she wasn't as dark-skinned as so many others around her. At a young age, she internalized this, and would feel the need to defend herself when people called her "negra." "Yo no soy negra," she'd say, "yo soy indiecita."

Catcalls scared her to her core, but they somehow were supposed to be flattering.

***

When a woman is promiscuous, she is shamed, while simultaneously being expected to be promiscuous. It's that thing that feministas call the Virgen/Puta dichotomy. Hay que ser una dama en la calle y una puta en la cama.

I remember one of the first instances of being shamed for my promiscuity. I was a teenager, 15, and living with the knowledge that everything was temporary at that point because at the end of the school year, my family was moving to New Jersey again.

I was returning from a school field trip to this water park called Kaskada, and the entire time, I had been flirting with this super cute guy. He wasn't from the school and came to the trip with his cousin who was one of my classmates and who I had low-key been talking to. The guy's name was Henry.

One moment, as I was chilling in my seat trying to look extra cute, one of my classmates stopped by. She maliciously whispered, "Tú eres una puta."

I remember feeling so ashamed that my entire mood changed for the rest of the trip. I silently let out two tears. My classmate wouldn't care that I flirted with his cousin, we weren't into each other anymore anyway.

So in the end, I went out with Henry anyways, but not without that moment getting to me.

At that age, for me, going out meant holding hands and kissing once or twice. You see, despite all of the over-sexualizing around me from older men and young boys, I was always expected to wait until marriage to have sex.

Our culture tells women that we must be good, and that "body count" matters. The number of partners we have matters. I knew this explicitly, though I didn't immediately see the problem with it.

It took me a while to get over this guilt and to begin to embrace "sexual freedom." And I use quotation marks because freedom doesn't go beyond an internal healing process. Meaning, I know that my "body count" doesn't matter and is completely irrelevant to my worth as a woman. While I have this knowledge now, our world sees otherwise. The discourse is that a woman's worth is based on her body and not her humanity, and that the owners of femme bodies are the social actors that consume them, the government that polices them, and the cis, hetero men who assault them.

As I began to learn more about my body and come to terms with my sexuality, the physical pain I actually felt during sex once I became active, also gradually went away. I also started to become interested in other women. I started feeling attracted to them as I soon as stopped seeing them as competitors or enemies, and as I started to learn to love myself too.

Though it wasn't until I studied abroad in Paris that I had my first adult sexual encounter with a woman. It was during a party at a club. I kept flirting with a very thin white woman, who was dancing by the DJ, and after a lot of eye contact, she finally came to the dance floor. We decided to go into the one-person bathroom stall, after making out in front of everyone.

After we got out of the bathroom, a man approached me and asked if I only liked women. I lied and said yes. He replied in French, "Tu as besoin d'un homme." He said this as he leaned on me, threateningly. I walked away from him, afraid. This was my first sexual encounter with a woman and here was this guy already threatening me by saying that I needed a man.

My intimate relationships with other women didn't go very far after that. I continued exclusively dating men for several years. Then, last year, when I started to consider dating women again – especially as I found myself having crushes on some of my queer friends – I was reminded of the very first encounter that I ever did have with sex.

***

The girl was someone who lived close by. The girl was 12 years old and she was seven. She would make her go down on her. She'd also lick her back, so it seemed mutual, though she barely felt anything. What she remembers most vividly was the girl telling her to go wash her face afterwards…the girl would yell at her if she didn't. One time, the girl brought one of her friends over and asked her to do it to her too. They all "did it" to each other. They would hide so that no adults would catch them.

She wasn't explicitly forced into it, but this girl was someone older, whom she feared. So maybe she was forced, but it's easier for her to assume that's not how it happened. At that age, she didn't even understand what was happening.

Because the other person was a girl who turned it into a sort of game, she never realized that it could be considered sexual assault until recently. She noticed it when she began developing a deeper interest in women. She was also in a comfortable and

47

safe place in her life; after years of being broke and very financially insecure post-college, she had finally gotten a descent a job.

But it was during those very days when different smells began giving her flashbacks to those moments. She felt immediately repulsed, like she could not be with other women. I mean, she wanted to puke and sometimes she did. She tried to shake the memory away but couldn't. And it kept happening again and again. Smells outside the bedroom reminded her of it. Those recollections were something that she had rarely even thought of before. It was a forbidden and shameful secret. Something to never bring up. And somehow, these were the very symptoms that she had read victims of abuse would experience: incredible shame, guilt, and the delusion that it was consensual. Though the girl too was a child. And she later learned the girl was also a victim of sexual assault at the hands of an adult.

***

Dominican culture is riddled with these secretos a voces: things that everyone knows are happening, yet no one discusses. And so are other communities of color. And so are other communities that aren't of color.

***

I was working at a summer camp. This was after returning from my anxiety-filled semester abroad in Paris. While I was abroad, I went into debt and also gained 40 pounds. Actually, when my sister's boyfriend at the time saw me, he even dared to say,

"Wow, it's like Liz has another sister."

I was humiliated. During this time, I developed an eating disorder. I literally felt that I couldn't live in my own body. So of course, escaping to the mountains of upstate New York was the solution — a job that I found solace in and that I did well.

When the camp ended, and we were left on camp grounds on our own to clean up, all of the counselors hooked up with one another.

At first, I refused to give in. I also got a lot of negative attention for being overweight, except for this one guy who told me that I was "thicker than a snicker." One day, another person – this random guy who had played another girl and who was a total dick – took notice of me. We were drinking, and I guess part of me told myself, "What the hell." He was the only one to take notice. So, I went into a room to have sex with him after several drinks. While I was giving him head, I got tired and told him that I was done and that I wanted to stop.

That's when he yanked my hair and whispered to my face, "You're gonna make me bust a nut," and he pushed me back down on him.

I knew that this was wrong. Yet I was basically forced to finish. I was terrified and felt like I had to. I had gone with him to the bedroom and had started to have sex with him. I couldn't just stop. Saying no wasn't an option. I mean, at least he didn't rape me with intercourse, right? That's what I told myself after. That night I stayed in bed with him and left early the next morning. He ignored me for most of the next day, and I was so hurt.

***

I have gone through a lot of shit during these past couple of years of being in my 20's. Still, I have prevailed and learned about self-love and self-care. I have also learned deeply about consent and what having safe sex looks like. Pero as a woman, I will only ever be relatively safe because of rape culture.

You see, rape culture is everywhere, not just in the very act of rape. It exists in the man who catcalls a woman as she walks down the street, in the telenovelas where it is even portrayed as flattering, in the lack of collective action around educating young children and adults about consent. It exists in the young girl who daydreams about male attention, even the bad kind, because she wants to feel beautiful.

Sí-guapa

Hopping on this beat
like una bacana
Piel de vaca pa la tambora piel negra pal alma
Si te agarro en la calle te jalo pa mi cama
Ven papi yo no muerdo
I guess tampoco duermo

Soy la jicama
Vamo a perrear en cuatro pata

Me dijeron que me cuidara
Que los hombre agarran a la mujere por atrá
Depué de la nalgá viene la puñalá
Y depué van a decir que lo merecí por andar
De cama en cama
Ahora hasta me toca andar armada
Que si pepper spray que si clase de defensa propia

Mi cuerpo un eje
Tus miradas matan.

When I had just arrived to the United States and was taking an exam at the high school to see how much English I knew, I wasn't the only one; there were about 20 students taking the test, and about half of us were Dominican. The other students were Central American or Colombian.

First, we took a written exam, then, when the teacher started doing the oral exam, she noticed about half of us were fluent.

She couldn't understand this back and forth that would put us in a position to be fluent, then leave, then come back pa coger este examen.

But I did. And knowing there were other students whose parents did the same as mine had made me feel like I wasn't alone.

When it came time to pick our class schedules, she put me in regular classes – for the most part.

Except for English. They didn't have space in the regular English classes, so she had to put me in English CP, which stands for college prep.

The entire thing felt so arbitrary. Like my future was being decided based on spaces. In the D.R. they'd fit us all in the grade we were in no matter what, for better or worse. Still, I was excited about being in an advanced English class. Over the years, and by that time, my English had really improved. Mostly because I had completed 8th grade in the U.S., since Mami tried to have us live in West New York that one time. But also because my tía sent me all types of YA books from the U.S., and I became an avid Harry Potter fan.

Still, once school started, it was a challenge. I had to work hard.

At the end of senior year, I was number six in the whole class, but they took me out of the ranking because they couldn't count the GPA for my first and second year of high school, since they were from the D.R.

The counselor told me this when I asked her why I wasn't included in the college visits the top students were in.

I felt invisible. I was so heartbroken. I cried for days.

All that hard work, those hours I put into staying a straight A student.[*]

At the time, it was also just my older sister and I living in the apartment next to my cousin. It was actually the same apartment where my parents lived when I was born, coincidentally.

Mami had moved back to the D.R., saying she didn't like it here. So, she left us behind and I had no one to really advocate for me. My sister was in college herself at the time – art school – and I couldn't stand her those days, because she'd try to boss me around. At 20 years old, she was forced to act like my mom and handle things around the house, from cooking to cleaning to making sure the bills got paid with her own job and cash Mami

---

[*]At Memorial H.S. I also did things I had not gotten to do in the D.R. yet. I got really drunk for the first time after downing close to half a bottle of agua ardiente. I started saying "yo" which my mom hated, but in the immigrant town we were in, I was surrounded by a different kind of English than the one from the white stories on Gilmore Girls and Friends I relied on in the D.R. — another face of America with more people like me. I also snuck out of the house to make out with some guy, and constantly lied about my whereabouts. I made out with a girl "for fun."

Los cristianos dirán que me dañè. Yo digo que me despojè.

sent from the D.R., and some child support from Papi. I also got a job at A & P. Still, I was mad because I just wanted a sister.

Getting taken off the class ranking also meant I wasn't going to be considered for any of the things that the top students enjoyed, like scholarships or more specialized counseling.

Tanta mierda pa na. I was una inmigrante.

Then, I got a call from the Ronald McDonald House of Charities Scholarship. My essay about moving to the United States won me a scholarship, and they were going to come with Telemundo to film a segment at the school. I even came out en *El Especialito*. As you can imagine, everyone was proud. "¡Amandita 'ta en el periódico!" My counselor came out in the paper talking about, "She's a great student."

It felt like I mattered again, all because I went out of my way (after Mami told me) to apply for this thing. Then, I got my acceptance letter to the Rutgers University Educational Opportunity Fund program. The McDonald's people weren't impressed by my school choice; I guess they thought I'd be going to an Ivy League school or something since they were giving me this $10,000 scholarship. My English teacher said I wasn't ready for a big school like Rutgers and told me I should go to a smaller place instead. Other students weren't impressed either. "Everyone gets into Rutgers," they said.

Still, I didn't give a fuck. I was ecstatic! When the yearbook came out the month before graduation, I was surprised to find my picture in the first few pages of the book.

The counselors had put me in the class ranking of top students again.

54

I bring a man home.

He's kind. He's timid but intelligent. His eyes are the warmest. They make me feel like home.

His smile defies the sadness in his eyes, like the last flame in a dark world.

Hair cut fresh, straight out the barbershop. Brown skin. Criado aquí, en Queens.

I ask what they think of him. Did they like him?

"Oh, you know he seems nice, a typical Dominican guy."

The words seem innocent, but I know what they mean. They don't see him. They see what they don't approve of. His hair. His skin.

He is everything they wish I already wasn't. And everything they don't want us to be.

The things about me that I now love the most because I love me. And I love him.

Un Haikucito

Yo soy perfecta
Pa que uté lo sepa
¿Entendió? Coño.

Cycle of Violence

I confronted him one time. I told him that I read something she wrote, where it said he touched her when she was very young.

People always tell me that that was some brave shit to do, but there's nothing to celebrate. I was sixteen, confused, and disgusted. And I wanted to rip my skin off because mi piel no puede ser su piel.

He said he doesn't remember. He laughed nervously; he said he wondered if maybe he was drunk.

My world collapsed when I found out and the guilt and shame felt like too much to bear.

I wanted to spare her. I wish it had been me.

I've been mostly living on my own since I started college right before turning 18.

I hopped between college dorms every year, like a nomad. Bargaining about where to spend Christmas or Easter. Getting rides from friends and my cousin when I'd go and visit my novio on the weekends or return to campus after summer ended.

Summers were spent in West New York with my sister. After college, I moved back in with my her. But I had to leave quickly. She had a boyfriend and had moved out of where Mami had left us and would always yell at me. It just wasn't home anymore.

The stress of not having money for rent when I moved out haunted me. I'd feel embarrassed to call my dad out of the blue to ask for money since I rarely spoke to him. One time I called my mom, sad, because I had no money. She started crying, saying it was her fault. Inundating the phone line with her sobbing.

There was no space for my sadness. I told her, "Nevermind." That I'm okay. That it's not her fault. That I'm okay and she doesn't have to cry.

I hung up and felt alone.

At the time, I found love in Shaun's arms.

Shaun. El gringo. Hip-hop artist and beautiful singer. One time, he wrote a song about hunger and told me it was about me.

Of course I believed him.

I could write a thousand words myself about our love. I guess that's not a lot.

58

But I almost died for that guy when I finally ended it.

He gave me validation with his visits. His kisses. We'd sing Jorge Drexler and Fito Páez together. I'd tell him I learned their music while hanging out with my sister's artist friends in the D.R., but I'd never give her full credit for it. He also loved when I read my poetry for him. Said it made him fall in love.

He had a girlfriend, but she was in Chile doing some activism work and I was his girlfriend for now. I mean, he had a toothbrush at my place and some clean clothes. We saw each other several times a week for an entire summer. And some of the winter.

He was about 10 years older than me. But to me, it was all a desperate romance between star-crossed lovers. We slept in my twin-size bed in my tiny studio apartment in Jersey City, where I was always a month behind on rent.

One time, we made love for so long, the sun came out, and we both looked outside like, "Damn, we just did that."

My studio had barely anything in it. No couch. No chairs. Just a twin-size bed and a few plastic drawers. The kitchen was tiny, practically closet-sized. I loved that the small bathroom had a real tub you could lay in.

Before moving in, I bought paint and had the super paint the walls yellow for me. What I was most proud of was this upside-down map that covered the wall down the length of my bed.

Even though the windows faced an alleyway and more windows, I bought sheer blue curtains so the sunlight could come in.

It was my home. My first real space. I was a whole-ass grown woman.

And with being a whole-ass woman came something else. Some men in the building who I lied to about living alone.

One who chased me on his bike when I went out for a run just that one time.

And my cousin's husband. This disgusting asshole started stalking me to the point where I had to file a police report. They lived two towns over. It all started with a message, right after Christmas. He texted me calling me a puta. I called him like, "Did you send this by mistake?" He said he didn't. After that, he doubled down. It was text after text after text after text after text professing his so-called love. In one of them, he said, "Yo sé que tú estás sola." In another voicemail, he said he'd come find me by Journal Square; he knew I lived in the area.

It all came out of nowhere.

I had never been so afraid in my life. I pictured myself becoming another dominicana murdered. Otro feminicidio. When I got home, I'd check around me when I left the train at Journal Square, while I walked up the stairs, behind the door in my apartment, in the bathroom. I'd cry the entire time, jumping at any small noise. I was terrorized.

When I finally went to my sister's place because I couldn't stand being alone, she laughed at me. "How could you be scared of him?" My mom told me that it's part of being a woman. My cousin (his wife) called him and told him I was going to call the police. My cousin didn't mean any harm; she's just stuck in a bad situation.

I told Shaun. He got angry. But that's all. What else could he do?

I left that studio and moved to Sunset Park in Brooklyn, with a young artist and woman whom I had met at a party, and a guy who was a designer who knew Shaun. Even though I was in New York City, my commute to work at a non-profit downtown was longer by about 30 minutes, but it was far from everyone. And the neighborhood had a street that reminded me of Bergenline Ave. and some activist and artist friends whom I had become close with. Above all, though, it was safe.

I picked the smallest room. I could barely fit everything in it. But it was cozy. And cheap. The room had no closet, so I bought an armoire. This time, I got a full-size bed. I'm a grown-ass woman now. I have sexual partners. I want to sleep right.

The room had just one window facing a busy highway. I could see the Hudson River and the tiny Statue of Liberty, very far away. The noise was the worst at first. Damn, why didn't we check out this apartment at night too? But eventually I got used to it, and the constant humming of the fast-moving cars helped me fall asleep at night.

I got sheer blue curtains this time too. And when morning came, the sun would rise right by that window.

Trigger Warning: HARRASSMENT

You get a text one night, from your cousin's husband. He's an asshole. The asshole of the family. You've always known this. But you think even this is unlike him. He starts off calling you a puta. And when you call him to ask if he meant to send that, he said, "Dije lo que tenía que decir." You don't know what to say. So, you dismiss it.

Then it starts. You keep getting text after text after text. One moment he says you're beautiful and that he loves you, and the next he calls you disgusting, saying you'll never love someone like him. Then he calls you a perra. Then he begs you to consider him as a partner. Then he says he knows you live alone.

The person seems delusional and starts texting you lies as well. That he knows you sent someone to threaten him: your boyfriend, even though you're single. Some texts don't make sense because he doesn't know how to write. This lasts about three days. Until the last day, when you're at your sister's place and your phone doesn't stop ringing. Also, for some reason, your phone can't block texts. This was 2014 and you don't have a fancy iPhone. You call your phone company and they can't do anything because they don't offer a "blocking service." You download a blocking app, which has to allow the phone to ring once before blocking. Finally. You call your phone company again. And change your phone number.

You don't tell anyone in your family what your new number is so he doesn't somehow end up with it. You go to the police station by your sister's place in Bayonne, NJ, alone, and tell the police what is happening. You start crying, then remember to be strong. You got this. You suck the tears in. You're taking action. You're not afraid anymore.

They say you can't file a restraining order because this person isn't your ex or someone you were in a relationship with. They say you can take them to court. But you're afraid that that is what this person wants. To see you. To bother you. To cause a reaction. To be instigated. You remember when he threatened you. "Llama a la policía. Llama que los estoy esperando."

While you're going to court, will you be protected? What if he retaliates?

You decide to just file a police report.

At least if you get killed, this will make him a clear suspect.

You try to file the report saying this person was harassing you. They tell you that you can't file a police report there; you can do it from where you live, in Jersey City. So, you leave. Crying. Without answers. Head home. To where you live. Alone.

When you go home, you call the police to file a report. The cops come over to your place. But you don't trust men, let alone the police. So, you meet them downstairs. They tell you this is awful. "If this was my daughter!" one said. You feel insulted again and again when you're asked again and again if you ever had any type of relationship with him. This man is disgusting. He's old as fuck. He's ugly as fuck. The whole family hates him. You all called him an ogre before you stopped mentioning him at all.

And now you can't help but feel like he won by harassing you enough that you even have to answer that question. "He's just delusional," you say.

"What did your family do?" They ask.

"What can they do?" You wonder.

One year later, someone strange shares your photo on Facebook. You go to the profile and notice it's him. He has photos of you on his page. Weird, random, cropped photos that seem to be from when you were very young. From family gatherings. You block him.

And the entire time, you think of the times you spoke to him nicely. He is your cousin's husband after all. Your second cousin's father. You think of the times you slept on your cousin's couch and wondered if he started his obsession with you then, when you started working in New York City and your sister's place was too far. You think of the time you left your make-up at your cousin's place and he said he'll "hold it for you." When you were a young teen, 15, 16, 17, 18, 19, and visited all the time. And spent Christmas in that apartment. Your cousin has never moved, unlike everyone else, so that home has been a constant in your life.

You think of the one or two times he helped you move in and out of college when your cousin picked you up in her car. She was the only one with a car. And he carried all your shit. Why were you ever nice to him? Why did you ever speak to him at all?

It's 2016, years since the whole shit started. Your sister is moving out. She lives with a cousin who decides to call him to help move. This time though, you don't give a fuck. You're ready. "Let me confront this asshole. Let me look him in the face," you think. He's huge. A fucking beast. But at least you'll fucking fight and go down with dignity.

You don't say this though, you say nothing. You act like you didn't notice. But everyone else who's there won't let you act like he isn't coming. They all silently panic, without saying anything out loud. Like they're hiding something from you. "Come with me. Let's go to the store." Your cousin takes you out and only brings you back when he's gone. You wonder, why are they so scared? Does he still talk about me or something?

It's New Year's Eve, 2018. You get a private message on Facebook and it's from him. It's like he'll never stop.

And through all this, you remember what your Mami said. She told you the story of how one time a man – a friend of her husband's when she was younger than you – was giving her a ride somewhere, and when he made a pass at her, she knew her husband wouldn't believe her account of the events, so she threatened to jump out of the moving car if this man didn't keep his hands away from her.

"Es parte de ser mujer," she told you.

You remember something your sister said when it all started, making you feel disgusted with yourself. "He respects me," she said, "cuz I never spoke to him. Yo siempre fui dura y distante con él." You can feel the blame in her voice. And you resent her for it, because your feminist self knows that's some bullshit. But a part of it still gets to you. And you can't help but feel disgusted with yourself for treating him like you do everyone else.

You don't treat men like everyone else. You don't smile at them when you say, "Good morning." You don't ask, "¿Cómo tú 'tá?" You don't make eye contact or polite conversation with them. You should've known; you don't treat men like humans. You treat them like the threat that they are.

Part 2

Mulata contemporánea searching for autonomy

Artist Statement: *When I take selfies, it feels like a performance for someone else, but calling it that would be too simplistic, when I take these photos and feel liberated somehow. I perform sexy and feel sexy; I perform femininity and feel feminine. In choosing the performance, I internalize it.*

I read that during the colonial era, they sent pictures of mixed-race women from el Caribe back to Europe. They called them mulatas. Their bodies, their faces, their features – they used these to make people interested in coming to the New World.

So, the settlers came.

And when I go to el Caribe, many times they call me the same thing they called those women.

Can I clean the oppression off? Can I rewrite the history of el Caribe, the history of colonization? Can I rewrite the history of my body?

"Sexy"
Se quisieron apoderar de mí
Se quisieron burlar de mí
Sequía en sus labios
Sectioning my body into pieces
Sexy su culo
Sexy sus tetas
Sexy sus labios
Sanctioning my freedom
Tú dices sexy
Sects sí
Yo digo
Sex sin dueño
Sex sí

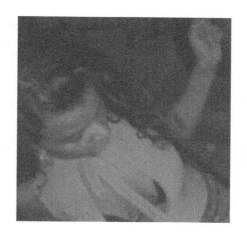

Memelo pun
Ay memelo pun
Memelo pun
Ay memelo pun
Así cantábamos cuando era niña
Memeleando
La canción era de mujere freca
"Se suben la faldita
Se le ve la popolita
Y los chicos se avergüenzan
Eso e mala ratrería"

Ahora estoy yo aquí
De ratrera
Déjalos que se avergüencen los chicos

Dedos entrelazados entre mi greña
Trapping lovers' fingers with the strength of the ancestors

Pero
Shea Moisture is too strong
Suave is too soft and it has sulfates
I'll settle for coconut milk
Pretending it'll do something, but it doesn't
Like wtf am I, a vegan dulce de leche?
It's like the new Caribbean woke casi-hipster-except-we're-poor wave
all about that sulfate-free-organic-energetic-brujería
que se vende en pote

Caribbean whiteness, that's my hair.
Creeping up in my head,
disrupting the curves,
rectificando todo,
reminding me I ain't shit if it weren't for its presence in my body

Medusa's serpents
The first sin of the Americas happened en el Caribe
Y quedé yo.

I remember when he taught me how to comb it
treat it with love for the first time
it's my crown
it's my black ancestors
it's...
it's glorious.
sin joyas
sin flores
Así, it's enough.

"taína"
Entre violación y muerte
Nació algo que nunca existió
Del blanco y negro
Un nuevo gris
Parecido a lo que dicen que ya no existe.

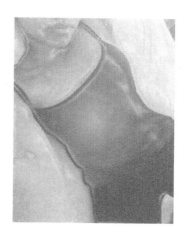

Snapchat
Snapchatting
Snapping shots of my real desires
Ephemerally alive
Like everything
Snapping me in half
till my respectability stops existing
and I pour my messy self onto your screen
Letting u snoop into my life
in loops of 5 seconds at a time
in this photo, I look like a bridge

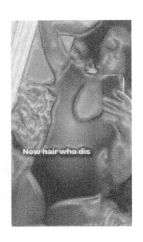

Me corté la melena
I'm not as melanated
but I'm melanating constantly

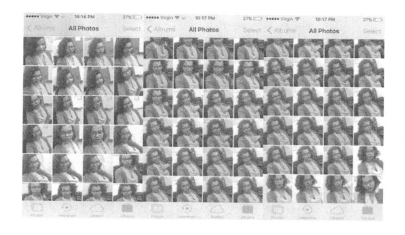

I cut my hair to stop hiding my face
Then I took 116 photos
To get a good shot

radical_latina   •••

Esta foto es la que tiene más likes de todas mis fotos
"La autenticidad vende"
Es por el gaze
Porque no estoy posando
Porque no tengo agencia visible
Eso es lo que la hace "auténtica"
Que no estoy de privona
Que no me digo bella
Y aun así se me ve tremendo cuerpazo

Caminando así mismo por la calle es que me gritan los hombres
Ni siquiera tenía los pezones llenos
Cuando comencé a coger el camino largo pa ir a la escuela
Pa que no me jodieran

Tus likes son los catcalls modernos
Pero, yo los pido, los elijo.
I ask for it.
Posting this photo is agency. Or is it an obligation?
A moral duty?
Potential likes would be wasted.
"You look so good in that photo – post it!"
Extending the gaze. Cuz I'm fly as fuck.
You're welcome.

"mulata"
Me dijeron mulata en la calle
Y sentí que en mi mismo vacío estaba la plenitud
De cualquier lado que me cojas
Me coges o por fetish hacia algo que consideras inhumano
o por odio hacia esa misma cosa
Soy inherentemente violencia anti-Negra y
en esa misma verdad es que se encuentra mi realidad de Negra.

Reguetonera Dreams

I wanted to write poetry, but instead I wrote a rap
Me van a decir that I can't cuz it's not my past
Dominican whiteness was my trap
So I can't possibly know rap
Black skin white masks
Our negritud was hacked
Solitude intact Solidarity inact

This is not an act

But I do pretend to be a bruja
Let candles light the way
Pray to my ancestors every day
So I won't keep being prey
I used to think catcalling was a praise
Only if I'm half naked do u say that I slay

I used to peel mangoes with my bare hands
Santiago niña still trying to get ahead
#SorryImNotSorry I'm not giving u head.

I used to think always saying sorry was my fate
I used to hide the rice and beans under the plate
Reguetón in my headphones on the subway
HTV couldn't whitewash this away
Writing rhymes in the mirror I'm Issa Rae
Insecure, hiding, I felt ashamed
So today I cut my hair to stop hiding my face.

Today I cut my hair to stop hiding my face.

I desperately want this story to be about sex and heartbreak. I want this story to be about Fernando, el fotógrafo who broke my heart so many times, yet I still let him be the first to visit me here. Or Héctor, el dominicano who swears we had a spiritual connection while he was on top of me, looking deeply into my eyes. "Nada más con mi novia me he sentido así," he would say.

Or about Chris, and how I almost went to Puerto Rico with him. Or about Mario, el niño lindo de Santiago, who surprised me when he offered to go down on me cuz los hombres de Santiago se creen muy finos para esas cosas.

But it isn't. Cuz you see, the same room where I made love with these men, I had stabbed myself on my inner wrist with the razor blade that I got from the pencil sharpener. It was so thin that it barely left marks, so sharp that it cut deeper and faster than the kitchen knife, and so small it felt innocent somehow — like it was okay. It became a nightly ritual; I would come home, anxiety-ridden, and play with how deep I would cut this time. Every cut confirming que yo no valía nada. I would hope that these guys would notice it. That they would ask about the blood stains on my bed, but they never did.

Instead, they marveled at how I decorated this tiny space: map on the wall of the world turned upside down, postcards of different places I'd been to hanging across the room con una cuerda, amateur paintings by me. And sheer blue curtains that let the natural light in and colorful sheets.

One night, I cut so deep I could no longer keep those sheets. My psychiatrist sent me to the hospital when I went to see her the next day.

Caribbean Bae

U were told so many times u weren't
beautiful
Or worthy of love

Chamaquita

Most times u believed it
Y ese sentimiento de ser inferior
Esa vaina de sentirte siempre niña
Slipped into ur smile
Making it look faint
Casi broken spirit
Casi broken
Casi broken into pieces of dust
From an existence, without being present

Waiting to finally be seen so that you could be poured into a
beautiful jar de mármol and be displayed forever, a perpetual
reminder of what could've been.

Today u look back at those days and think
I survived
Pendejos.

Dear Diary,

I bought 4 books today. And an oil. And herbs. I'm going to heal for real this time. And men won't be my downfall. And I'm going to be amazing. I'm going to start a vlog, and get writing fellowships. And I'm going to dance my ass off. And dedicate so much love and energy to myself. And maybe no man will be able to handle me. Because I'd have to suppress myself. Maybe it's gonna hurt. Maybe I'll regret breaking up with him. Leaving the home we were building. But I also know when I think of us that that shit hurt. That it hurt tremendously. That I wasn't happy. That I was yearning for something. And I lived in yearning. And he will be fine. He will be fine. He will be fine. He will be fine. Maybe he wants me. Maybe. Maybe he does. Maybe he'll change and come find me. Or maybe I'll be left yearning that he will. But I only have one life. You only have one life Amanda. One life.

He will have kids with another woman and make them happy and they will be happy and it'll be fine. It'll be beautiful and dope. And maybe you won't meet someone else but you'll be good. You can have a baby like Liz and be a single mom and love that baby so much. And you can have sisters. And you can garden with old ladies and you can live with old ladies and be free.

Learning how to make té pa'l mal de amores

Maybe these rose petals will be enough to cure me.

Los echo uno a uno, supposedly blessing them as I drop them into the pan with hot water. "Mi intención con este té es quitarme este mal de amores," I whisper. I say supposedly because what power do I have? I'm no santera. I haven't been baptized or invited into any spiritual practice, at least not since my non-consensual Catholic one when I was a baby. All I have are candles that I light sometimes to San Miguel, sometimes to Mother Earth, sometimes to Anacaona, sometimes to a combination of saints, praying but not too hard so as to not disturb them with my ingenuidad. I remember you asked me about this when you saw the makeshift altar in my room.

Mi abuela on my dad's side era curandera – at least that's what my dad told me. She died when he was in his early 20's while he was attending la Universidad Autónoma de Santo Domingo — the first one established by the colonizers in the Americas. And so, when I drop these petals into this tea, I think of her too. I try to remember what she was never able to teach me. I think of how her hands must've been: were they soft and gentle? Or rough from hard work? I picture su casita en el barrio de Pueblo Nuevo. You know, I only recently saw a picture of her for the first time.

Yo también quiero ser curandera. O naturalista. O yerbera.
Like her. Though I bet she didn't have a name for it.

I actually need to become like her in order to survive. I'm living this simulated life in this simulated city where I build altars in cold concrete corners, away from my home country, and where it's fucking cold. So, I've been teaching myself. I imagine her fingers could trace cures by feeling the leaves; mine need to type questions into keys to hopefully get a proper response from Google.

Papi said que la gente venía de todas partes a buscar remedios donde mi abuela. When he told me this, my uncle gave him a side eye. Clearly, él 'taba exagerando. But I didn't care, I believed him. And now, feeling the salt pouring from my eyes into my lips, I pray to her so that somehow her magic can be transferred to me, at least to make this tea. Did I inherit her gift?

I wish I could tell you this story, but you stopped texting me back. I cut the ginger into thin slices. I know I'm supposed to guayarlo, but I'm too tired, so I just throw the chunks into the pot. The ginger will desintoxicar mi cuerpo, and hopefully help release the toxins from under my skin where you seem to be stuck. I go to my window, where I have basil growing...She had a garden; I have my fire escape. Basil, they say, is to get rid of bad energy. As I stir this mix, I think of how I traced your body with my fingers too, regalándote caricias que se perdieron somehow en tu brown skin. Y por ahí perdí yo la cabeza. This must be why they call it "mal de amores." Before the "mal de amores" that you gave me, I had dique "winter blues." For a moment, I thought breathing your scent was my cure. Like lavender brings me peace, el olorcito que venía desde tu cuello, justo detrás de tus orejas, me hacía sentir un poco menos el dolor del frío.

The last ingredient is honey. I make Mami, who still lives in the Dominican Republic, bring me one or two bottles of honey whenever she visits. It's pure, straight from el campo. My favorite part is cleaning the residue around the lid with my finger and licking it right after I seal it, so that it doesn't stay sticky.

My resistance goes beyond being alive
There're rhymes in my tongue that'll stay when I die
Like time
La diáspora Negra es inmortal
They proved it when they survived the sin
for which they never apologized

My resistance goes beyond being alive
Because my body is their shrine
In my dance is their fight
In my walk is their guiar
I tattooed the sun on my hips on a painful night
When me and my friends cried
Because of the hurt predators, abusers, rapists, stalkers were causing in
our lives
I guess somehow, I knew the sun was mine
in my hips there're birth rites

Circling through Mother Nature, her love is my right
I am filled with light
My grandmother died before I knew which questions to ask and
somehow, on my face, she still shines
If they lived so long after they died, so will I
My resistance will go beyond being alive

My last heartbreak

Heartbreak feels like
Joie de vivre
La misma capacidad de ser feliz es la misma de ser triste. Así es
el balance.

When my heart aches, nectar comes from my eyes
I have to learn to weave my heart together.

This time, though, it feels different
Like this pain is connecting me to something greater

If I can feel so much pain
So alive
So tender
Then God must be real.

She is here.

This pain, this ability to feel pain, this self-awareness

Is our curse.

But also what makes us feel like we're
little gods chillin'.

El dolor es la enfermedad
Y también la cura.

The psychiatrist saw my tiny scar. It wasn't even a real thing. I tried making it real. I tried cutting deep. But that shit hurts.

She saw it, and immediately called an ambulance to come get me. We were in Brooklyn. By the beach. I don't even know what hospital it was.

I had a feeling this would happen. Maybe I wanted it.

She had a thick Russian accent, big red hair. She was cool, quick, and to the point. Online, a lot of the reviews said this was just a place where people got their prescription refilled.

During my last visit to see her, I told her that the medication was reducing my libido. That sex wasn't that good. She told me that was probably better.

"You're a Latina, so sexy, maybe it's good that it goes down from 95% to like 85."

There are few moments where I recognized discrimination right when it happened, as opposed to noticing the aggression later, while reflecting on it. This was one of those moments.

But I didn't say anything.

She had prescribed two meds: one antidepressant and one that was for when I was having an anxiety attack. It helped me calm down, rocked me to sleep. But it was strong so I could only have half at a time.

I took my prescription and kept it moving.

The next time I was in for a regular check-up, I told her I wasn't feeling okay. Showed her my tiny scar on my left wrist. It's still there. She said that's not okay. And she quarantined me until an ambulance came.

They took me. With my barely-there scar.

The EMT guy reminded me of this guy I liked in college who wouldn't look at me twice. A popular on-campus athlete. We were just talking, regular stuff. How can a pretty girl like you be sad? What are you sad about? Do you have a boyfriend?

He got my number. We flirted. He dropped me off at the hospital. Helped me get signed in. And left.

They put a colorful bata on me. Apparently, I needed to wear this one and not the regular one cuz this one signified I couldn't leave at will.

They asked if I wanted to see anyone, alert anyone. Asked for any emergency names. I gave them none. A sweet nurse came by later and asked again. I gave them none.

Why are you hurting yourself?

I don't know I don't know I don't know.

You don't look sad, she says. Let me see your arm.

One time, during an appointment with my psychiatrist before the hospital visit, they had to check my heart. The reason was to make sure it was functioning well, so that the meds were safe.

I saw it on the screen. I took a video of it too. It was beating loud. Making squishy noises in between. Squeesh. Squeesh. Squeesh.

It was there. Beating away. After all the pain, heartaches. The betrayals. The dark shit. The violence. There it was.

Squeesh. Squeesh. Squeesh.

The doctor took some notes on her pad, then looked at me and said my heart was okay.

JOY

Love feels like joy. It rests at the end of the breath when your lungs are filled. That's why laughter takes your breath away. It's the full expression of letting out that joy.

I've always been told I laugh too loud. Around the right people, my laugh is embraced. Others have told me to keep it down. Like the laughter is just too much. How dare I be this happy. Fill the room with a shriek of joy.

We're more accustomed to the shriek of pain from women, and to overlook it.

Ive been embracing laughter more. Letting go of stress more. Saying "no" more. Saying "yes" to myself more.

Give me your laugh and I will use it as a seed to grow a tree and repopulate the Earth.

"Chula"

He called me chula. Our legs would be intertwined, and he'd just say it in between conversations. "Sí, chula." And in our text exchanges. "Hola Chula."

I loved that shit.

It just made the butterflies in my stomach somehow rise to my chest, make me smile. I felt sexy but also loved, in the midst of our Dominican New York love that crossed the bridge to Jersey, the word came with a warmth I couldn't describe. He's a photographer, just for fun, and he always took the best shots, probably because of those butterflies: La piel me brillaba. I wanted to be with him just to have an unlimited source of photos. "Chula, voltéate, ahora sonríe."

Yes, call me chula, please.

The word is cute. Pero yó a él lo boté. At first, I didn't wanna be with him. Then he never wanted to be with me, and eventually I found out it's cuz taba enamorao de una blanquita que duró pal de años pa hacerle caso. Meanwhile, I was always there, and whenever I ended any relationship with some new guy, he was always there too.

"Chula"

I'd whisper to myself posing in front of a mirror, poking my butt out. The last time I was single, I loved posting thirst traps. I wasn't hooking up with anybody, but showing off my sexiness made me feel alive again. En un momento tuve que parar; soy una periodista seria.

Esta gente no me va a tomar en serio si me la paso poniendo fotos lindas. Pero when I do choose to share, it's worth the risk.

"Chula"

Me volví sirena. En una de las Playas del Este, en La Habana. El taxista who gave me the ride me dijo que no me metiera muy lejos. But the sea held me. Sola. Free.

"Chula"

La foto mía de niña, con el pelo amarrado para atrás, with the little butterfly clips we all wore at one point…muy 90's. I began using this photo in presentations when I started taking performance seriously. Es que me veo tan chula en esa foto; I was a beautiful child, with soft eyes, and a lot of energy. I wrote my first poem when I was nine, around the time the photo was taken. So much love desde chiquita.

"Chula"

I looked up what chula means originally, hoping it was una vaina bacana. Pero na, it's some European shit. Whatever. We make everything our own and make it better – no jodan.

"Chula"

I find myself in you today. Mi niña chula y cariñosa. Belleza. You are so worthy of warmth. Of love. And you are enough. And you are whole. And chula, it's okay to feel whatever you're feeling. Be gentle with yourself.

And I do hold myself, and I spend more time at home, and I drink more water, and I've been learning how to twerk properly, and how to cook for me, and how to do the loud bird whistle with my hands so that if I'm ever lost again, I can find my way home.

Chula as fuck. Chulería en pote. Chuleandome a mí misma. La más chula.

"Chula"

How amazing is it to give ourselves butterflies?

I feel like I'm floating
There are needles in my forehead and my right ear. La mujer dijo
que eso era un punto de qué sé yo qué o qué sé yo quién.

I remembered how I tried searching for a mom in Yemayá y
Oshún; it don't work. And yes, that shit is all real. But it has
never worked for me.

I feel like I am floating, and I am somehow face-to-face with my
consciousness.

"¿Y tú que haces aquí?"
"Te tenía que hablar."

She's been here since she was a kid.

A baby.

"Tú ha pasao mucha mierda."

I didn't realize how much.

It feels like if I was. I am.

Ever floating in my head. Maybe we are trapped in our bodies.

But will we lose it all if we lose our host?
This house?
Esta casa.

I search for a home for my soul beyond my body cuz other
spiritual practices with bodies like mine aren't for me.

Yet. Or not yet.

Feels like another rejection. I can dance to palo. Muy bien too. Everybody's Mami seems to have had an altar y la mía no tenía na de eso.

I was born el día de San Miguel y nadie se acordó de ponerme Amanda Miguel.
Mejor así; I'm named after me, sino, hubiera salío acomplejá por cantar feo.

I went to Dajabón and met women who told me I was special.

Antes de ir a Dajabón, en la Frontera, I had a dream where I saw someone dancing in green, or purple, or blue – I always forget – inviting me in. In a place before the D.R. was the D.R. And the only place that is neither that and yet all of that is la Frontera.

I went to Cuba.
And danced in Havana. Con una gente que da clase ahí.

Y quise ser la mejor. Como siempre. Como en la escuela cuando me fajaba por una "A." I wanted them to somehow stop me and say I'm meant to follow this or that spiritual path.

Pero nada me sirvió.

I look into your eyes and I see you.

Me. You.

They say when we think back to early childhood memories, we see them in third person. But I know you're still here.

***

You were so cute. Your little, brown, skinny face. Your legs. They'd tell you that you had canillas like your dad. I don't know when you started living in your head. But you created a fantasy there. Creaste un mundo entero donde fuiste libre, salvaje, niña. Donde los errores eran permitidos. Donde nadie te gritaba, nadie te decía que hablaras más despacio, que por qué no eras más linda, que tenías que cambiar, que you were broken.

Una de las cosas más chulas, y de los recuerdos that always come back when I visit what used to be your home, was the little flowers that were in the front yard of la casa de Tía.

I was in Puerto Rico recently, writing this book, and ahí estaban. I googled the name. Se llaman Cruz de Malta. También se llaman Coralillo. That's my favorite name so far.

You'd play with your friend Rosy. And whoever else was around. I tried to remember how to play with them. My hands are much bigger this time, my fingers less delicate than when I was you. But still, I remember.

This was a self-love ritual. Your first one.

With your tiny hands, you rip a bunch of the flowers; they already came in bunches, so it was easy to rip them that way.

And you take one tiny flower one by one, from the bunch, desde el tallo.

With the flower in your hand, the first thing you do is push the yellow pollenated tip that's at the top, sticking out through a tiny hole. This tip is usually orange and powdery. You push it down, and from the other end of the flower, the stick would come out.

You pull the stick gently, once it's completely out. There's one single drop of nectar in the tiny hair-like stick. You lick it.

It's sweet, right? That's the reason you push it out and pull, instead of pulling straight from the orange top. Para que tengas el nectar para ti solita.

You set this flower aside, and you do that with another one. Once you have enough flowers, you can start connecting them from the end of one to the other, until you have a cord of flowers. Then, once you are satisfied with the length, you connect the two ends to make a necklace. You need about 6-7 flowers for a bracelet, 10 for a necklace.

And you'd wear it, you and your amiguita. They were so delicate you couldn't move around much cuz they'd break.

But you looked so beautiful.

***

I wake up from this non-sleep meditation to the lady's cold hands pulling one of the needles out from my foot. She takes them out one by one until she gets to my forehead.

It was so nice seeing you.

Aprender a quererte así, esa es mi religión.

Dear Diary,

Hi! How are you?? Hope you are great. Well, I know I am.

You see, I won the medal for being the best student. They also gave me a medal for winning first place in the Math olympics.

On the other hand, I don't know what's going on with me because I feel as if I'm tired of Carlos. And I know I'm not, and that I love him...he's my first real boyfriend! But I feel as if he was going to ruin my future and even though he probably won't, I feel like he is because since I'm with him and I'm going to be with him all this time, I feel as if when he finally moved to Santiago from La Vega, we would never break up because I gave him the best years of my life. And then after I get out of college, I will have to marry him right away because he will be old already. So I wouldn't be able to travel unless it's with him, and I don't mind but what if he won't want to. And since he's already older, he'll be very old by then, we would want to have kids and I will not be able to do all the things I want to. So what can I do besides end it? I mean really.

---

*14 years old, one year before moving to the U.S.

Call me Matitina
escandalosa desde niña
la más chula y la más linda

De adulta una conscious gentle diva
tú te creerás Dios
Pero yo por hombre no me pongo de rodilla
Si la más puta, soy la más fina

Travel the world with red lipstick
International caperucita
Que bellos mis ojos y grande mi sonrisa
Speak in three tongues
Parselmouth boquita
Si te pica es mi mariquita
A A A E E E
Esta es mi dicha
Bebiendo Country Club
y ganando la partida

Santiago meets the world en mis pupilas
I'm a pupil, maestra y la enseñanza misma
Escribiendo desde chiquita
Imma have to put this on Genius
Porque ta caliente la tinta

Dirán que soy privona
esta es mi vida
La vivo como una tigra

Y este cuerpo es mi casa
Y aquí Amanda es la que manda
Y esta es mi real patria
A ella le canto himnos
Mi bandera mi cara
Mi nutrición la lavanda

Riquezas por dentro
Ellos quieren robarla
mis ancestros me aguardan

Y no me digas mamacita
hasta que sea madrecita
Soy bonita y te gano en Jeopardy
Porque soy lista
Radio Bemba de noticias
Escuchando música y de cuentista
Antillana y Caribeñista

Vendiendo Empanadas Dita
Autonomía bendita
Con mis hermanas, toy activa
Y pa lo que venga: Guía ¡Siempre lista!

Buelita's Songs

Mírala que linda viene
Mírala que linda va
Con su vestidito rojo
Y la nalguita pa'trás.

The song went something like that. Though I can't remember if it's "vestidito rojo" or "vestidito corto." But when I listen to it, these memories that feel intensely mine pop up.

But I can't tell if I'm remembering them or if I'm imagining them.

I picture me with a cute little dress, a baby, as Buelita twirls me around. Her raspy voice singing this song. Telling me I look super cute in red.

Cada vez que pienso en ti y en estos detalles me dan ganas de llorar. She helped raise me for the first three years of my life, before I was taken to the Dominican Republic. Cuando Mami iba a trabajar en McDonald's.

Duérmete mi catirita
Duérmete mi catirita
Duérmete mi catirita
Que tu mami no 'ta aquí

That's another song. And I remember the warmth of her hands as she rocked me quickly to sleep singing this. El calor de tus manos firmes y a la vez arrugadas es el primer recuerdo que tengo, y que tierno es recordar algo tan amoroso.

My grandmother passed away the day after I graduated college. Mami was in the country for the occasion, and we took the opportunity of all of us being together to go visit her. She was in a hospital room after having had another stroke. She couldn't speak y estabas con la mirada perdida. Before leaving the room, I gave her a kiss on the forehead and

98

she smiled. Mami said, "She recognized you." And shortly after we left.

My graduation was wonderful – the second in our generation after my sister, the first on my dad's side. Then, I got the call. Alida passed in her sleep.

I didn't cry. I didn't feel anything. I was numb. I understood that she waited to see us all and waited for my graduation to pass. Still, there's never a right time for this. Back then, I also didn't understand how big of a loss that was. Tus manos cálidas se habían ido sin yo misma haberme dado cuenta de lo que habías significado para mí.

Eso fue en el 2012. Y desde hace quizás dos años después de eso, cuando me vi fríamente sola, con miedo, sin rumbo, comencé a buscarte. Me hice unos exámenes de ADN dique para saber más de donde venimos. Te hacen escupir en un frasquito, y después uno lo manda por correo, y por internet ve el resultado. No aprendí tanto de lo que buscaba, pero creo que te hubiera interesado saber que nuestra línea matriarcal (o sea la mamá de tu mamá de su mamá y así sucesivamente) viene de las Islas Canarias. Dique, porque uno nunca sabe con esos éxamenes. Para mí, al final, mi línea matriarcal, eres tú.

He tratado de encontrarte también en historias de nuestra familia. Me senté con tu hermana Subida para hablar de ti, de como eras. Y me contó muchísimo y a la vez muy poco. Tuviste mucho coraje Buelita.

I also heard that she used to work assisting at an abortion clinic in the 60's or 70's, something like that. Which I found so cool but risky. Rescuing our family history has been so difficult; it's like no one cares. What matters is who was from Spain and who had money. Inevitably those stories end up being about men.

I wanted to know about the women.

También traté de encontrarte en religiones que no se sienten mías. Mi tía me dijo que teníamos una pariente que era bruja, so a mí me cogió con averiguar quien era esa mujer. Que hacía en el bosque de noche. De dónde venían las prácticas que me contó Tía que ella hacía. And I googled and googled for hours trying to find what type of practices aligned more with the clues I'd been given about this bruja. And I came up empty-handed.

Es que he sentido este vacío por dentro. Un vacío espiritual, y un vacío humano. Como que no entiendo por qué estamos aquí. Y traté de buscar mi valor y el sentido de la vida en el pasado. ¿Alguna vez sentiste eso?

Liz has a baby, un niño super lindo. Un día, Mami le dijo "catire," porque supuestamente esa palabra venezolana es una que tú usabas, y significa niño rubio, o algo así.

Y me acordé de la canción.

Duérmete mi catirita
Duérmete mi catirita

Siempre pensé que Catirita era el nombre de una niña, pero catirita era otra cosa.

Y me dí cuenta que te buscaba en el pasado más allá del tuyo, más allá de cuando te conocí de baby, de adolescente, y al hacer eso, me imaginaba a otra persona, una ilusión de ti.

I asked my aunt about her and these songs she used to sing me as a kid. "Where did they come from?" My tía didn't know, but she said, "Ella siempre te cantaba canciones y a veces decía, 'hoy Amanda parece una flor.'"

"Lord she sang a lot of songs to you. She used to say when you would come over to the house, '¿A qué te pareces hoy Amanda? Pareces una rosa' and she'd dress you in red.
Or she'd say you looked like some flower of sorts, or a color. She always said you look like a white rose too. Other days she would say, 'No, rosada, hoy está vestida de rosada.'"

She also told me you would make up songs for me.

Es como si no me diera cuenta de lo mucho que me querías hasta ahora. Y me sentí avergonzada por extrañarte tanto cuando solo compartí contigo los primeros años de mi vida. I still felt this connection, so I searched for her desperately. Recently, I decided to look up these songs. I looked up the song "Mírala que linda viene" first to try to see if that gave me clues about your history. And I found out it's a Cuban song, something old from Carnival, inherited from ancestral Congolese traditions (depending on who you ask). Finding the history is hard. Eventually, I found out people in Puerto Rico sang it too, as a plena with different variations.

"Mírala que linda viene/Mírala que linda va/Es la novia más bonita que se acaba de casar."

"Mírala que linda viene/Mírala que linda va/La revolución boricua que no da ni un paso atrás."

I laugh at how it arrived at my house. En Puerto Rico, hablan de que la revolución no da un paso atrás, en una de las versiones cubanas también se menciona una comparsa, y en mi casa es de tener la nalguita pa'trás.

Ahora veo que eso de que te inventabas canciones debió ser verdad. De eso se trata la plena, y muchísimas otras tradiciones caribeñas, de improvisar. Y cuando me cuidabas solita en casa, estas canciones eran para mí.

Cuando escucho a Celia Cruz, o algún bolero, también me acuerdo de ti. Te gustaba cantar toda clase de música en la casa. Mami me dijo que te gustaba el flamenco. Y Buelita, yo también soy así. Escucho de todo. Y le canto a mi sobrinito también, y no fue hasta que me puse a escribir esto que me di cuenta que quizás lo aprendí de ti.

I was caring for my nephew the other day, and he was having a hard time falling asleep. So, I sang one of my favorite songs for him, which I've been singing to him since he was born. It's a ballad performed by Christina Aguilera, which I recently found out was originally a Cuban bolero called "Contigo en la Distancia." I sang while rocking him, y el carajito se durmió rapídisimo desde que comencé a cantarle y después de retorzar por varias horas.

Buelita, a veces nos complicamos tanto. Traté de aprender de ti buscando información sobre el campo donde vivías, creando un árbol familiar con tu apellido. Y sólo necesitaba verte a ti, lo que hacías, las cosas que te gustaban, y como cantabas por toda la casa. Aferrarme a tu voz y entender que no debía buscar fuera de ti para saber sobre ti.

That warmth of her hands was my spiritual baptism; they themselves were the tradition she passed down. It's like magic, but it's tangible. If I breathe deeply when I think of her, I can feel her warmth. What a blessing that it is my first memory on this Earth.

And somehow, with these songs, she did leave me a legacy too.

Mi canción favorita de todas es la de Matitina.

Yo no sé si conoces el origen de esta, ¡pero es chulísimo Buelita!

The history of this next song is surprisingly well-documented too.

Titina was the nickname of a woman named Antonia. On November 12, 1894, she shocked all of Havana riding her bike. She was the first woman to do so in public, and this song was actually created to mock her.

But Titina rode on. Despite the burlas, ella montó su bicicleta por Cuba. Y así hicieron otras mujeres. Cuando la canción vino a llegar a mí, ya se había vuelto "Matitina."

In these songs, there's also a history: one of el Caribe – not just las Antillas – but the Venezuelan coast, too. There was a time when we all sang each other's songs, más allá de lo comercial. Y tu viviste ese tiempo, esa época. Estas canciones llegaron al campo de Laguna Prieta, donde creciste, y de ahí me las diste a mí en West New York. Y eso te lo agradezco tanto...el darme estas canciones, y el quererme como me quisiste. De cierta manera, te siento aquí.

Matitina was my nickname as a kid because of this song, and some people still call me that. And whenever I went anywhere when I visited family in the U.S., they'd ask me to sing it. "¡Matitina! ¿Cómo es que dice la canción?"

And I loved singing it, I felt so much pride and loved to have an audience to hear me. I'd get excited especially because of the laughter that always came at the end, since the entire thing is actually kinda funny. Con una sonrisa grandísima, without blushing, I'd part my little lips and sing,

"Matitina Matitina
montando bicicleta
dobla la esquina
se le cayó la teta."

Outro

Dear New Diary,

Hi! My name is Amanda Alcántara Burgos, I'm 15 years old and I live in the Dominican Republic with my mom and my stepdad. I also have a sister but she moved to the U.S.

There are many things that I love to do and many things that I *would* love to do. I love to talk, make new friends, make out, read, write, dance, listening to music, going out with my friends, eating, watching TV, being a girl scout, learning, helping, being there for people, being called on the phone, winning and participating in things, studying, going to school, shopping, etc. etc. etc.

I would love to be happy, travel, learn how to dance merengue and salsa, change something in people, change the world, or at least the D.R. I love many things, but there isn't much that I hate. I am very good academically, that is something you should know, for example, recently I won for the 2nd time in a row the Math Olympics (first place) and last year I got a medal, but this year I will get a medal and a book. Even though it isn't such a big gift, I earned it so it is good enough for me.

I am also a very good Guide Scout (Guía Scout), and I was going to form my own group here in La Lotería, but I don't know if I will be because I'm leaving to the U.S. in August to do my Junior and Senior year of high school over there. Even though part of me doesn't want to leave, and nobody knows except for Mami and me.

About guys, right now there isn't anyone I'm dying for, I mean I would like to make out with some guys I like, but no relationships, which is good because I'm leaving. Well, I guess I'll tell you more later, because I have to go to school for my weekly scout meeting.

BYE ♥

Amanda Alcántara is a writer and journalist. Her work has appeared on NPR's Latino USA, Remezcla, The Huffington Post, The Washington Post's The Lily, BESE, and The San Francisco Chronicle. She has also been published in the anthology Latinas: Struggles & Protests in 21st Century USA, by Red Sugarcane Press. In May of 2017, Amanda obtained a Master of Arts from NYU in Latin American and Caribbean Studies, where her thesis focused on the experience of women residing on the border of the Dominican Republic and Haiti. Amanda is also a co-founder and previous editor of La Galería Magazine. Since 2018, she has been working as the Digital Media Editor at Futuro Media Group. She has a BA from Rutgers University. A map of the world turned upside down hangs on her wall.